The Simple Potty Training Handbook

+ 25 Great Tips To Help You Feel Confident & Prepared.

© Copyright 2019 - All rights reserved.

The content contained within this book may not be reproduced, duplicated or transmitted without direct written permission from the author or the publisher.

Under no circumstances will any blame or legal responsibility be held against the publisher, or author, for any damages, reparation, or monetary loss due to the information contained within this book. Either directly or indirectly.

Legal Notice:

This book is copyright protected. This book is only for personal use. You cannot amend, distribute, sell, use, quote or paraphrase any part, or the content within this book, without the consent of the author or publisher.

Disclaimer Notice:

Please note the information contained within this document is for educational and entertainment purposes only. All effort has been executed to present accurate, up to date, and reliable, complete information. No warranties of any kind are declared or implied. Readers acknowledge that the author is not engaging in the rendering of legal, financial, medical or professional advice. The content within this book has been derived from various sources. Please consult a licensed professional before attempting any techniques outlined in this book.

By reading this document, the reader agrees that under no circumstances is the author responsible for any losses, direct or indirect, which are incurred as a result of the use of information contained within this document, including, but not limited to, — errors, omissions, or inaccuracies.

Table of Contents

Introduction

Chapter 1: Before You Begin

Chapter 2: Other Preparation

Chapter 3: Starting

Chapter 4: Afterwards

Conclusion

25 Bonus Tips

Introduction

So… you're at that point. After doing lots of thinking, watching closely for telltale signs, casually asking friends for their advice, and growing more and more fed up with the messiness and high cost of disposable diapers, you've arrived at the decision – it's time. Time to start potty training!

And then, only seconds later, a whirlwind of questions began to cycle through your mind. How's it going to work? Where are you going to find time? How will you go about each crucial, practical step? Somehow, what seemed like a simple thing at first glance, suddenly started to look like a confusing, overwhelming obstacle.

You got online, did some searches, and maybe even watched some Youtube videos. Great job. Those are all worthwhile methods of gaining helpful information. But then it occurred to you… wouldn't it be nice to have a book full of tips that tried to combine as much helpful information together so that you didn't have to refer to a thousand different sources? And, that's what led you here. Again… great job!

This book aims to add value to your life by equipping you with knowledge and confidence about all you'll be facing. We'll talk about what you need to get started, how to handle different stages of the process, as well as dealing with certain issues that may arise – even after your child has been potty trained. We'll talk about the necessary equipment you'll need and give you plenty of tips to make you feel ready.

Wait… why are you laughing? You don't feel ready? Ok, fair enough. Let's face it… this is something that you may never feel ready for. But, it's also something there will never be an ideal time for, and you could easily put it off too long. So, one more time… good job. It's wise of you to begin this process as soon as you (and your child) are ready – regardless of how you feel!

In a way, this is a lot like when your child was born. Remember how consumed you were back then about the planning and preparation involved? You read books, listened to podcasts, and even asked your parents for their advice (which is something you thought you'd never do). You became a well-oiled machine. An encyclopedia with arms and legs, ready for just about anything life might throw at you. Yeah… you were ready!

Sure, a lot of that stuff may have gone out the window now, as your main focus revolves around figuring out what to put on the dinner table, as well as composing carpooling strategies that work with you and your family's busy schedules.

Maybe it feels strange to be back behind another steep learning curve, but that's natural. Every stage of your child's life comes with new learning curves and surprises. Each step along the way requires a break from your old thinking, as well as an adaptive mindset.

You are bound to feel a certain amount of stress. You'll be playing the roles of teacher, trainer, and guide. There is a lot at stake. This is an important period in your child's development, and it has the potential to grow his trust and confidence, or to be something that discourages you both. If you don't have a basic strategy, you could easily miss out on making the most of this opportunity.

The good news is that this can be a happy, pleasant experience for both of you. The language you use, the way you mentally prepare yourself, and the knowledge you gain about common mistakes will all make the whole process smoother.

When you hear that small voice calling for you at 3:00am, and you find a wet bed that needs new sheets and blankets, you may not respond perfectly, but you'll at least be somewhat prepared. You'll be more likely to see such small setbacks as the stepping stones they are, and to pick up right where you left off with a strong, positive attitude.

So, without further ado… let's dive in!

Chapter 1: Before You Begin

What You Should Know

Having a baby brought a lot of extra baggage—both literally and figuratively. Every corner and flat surface seemed to fill up with necessities. Diapers. Wipes. Butt cream. Diaper Genie®. A changing table. Portable changing pads. They occupied all the space in your bags, next to your bed, under the crib, and in the closets. These things became so commonplace that you actually found it hard to think you'd ever stop needing them.

Take a deep breath (And yes, someday that breath will no longer be tainted by the smell of a dirty diaper). After only a short time, you'll soon be looking back and wondering where on earth this time went. You'll wake up and see a child that's bigger and more independent. You will look back almost sadly, missing those moments when it was so common to look in your child's eyes as she lay on the changing table.

The timing for every kid is different. Just as you can't decide when she will start walking or talking, you also cannot place a deadline on when she'll be ready for potty training. How can you tell if your child is ready? That usually becomes evident when she starts showing curiosity about how the toilet works, putting on underwear, and wanting to use the potty. Her emotional and physical development largely determine her readiness.

Some children begin to express interest around the age of 2, while others don't show any until they are at least 3. Though there are no exact guidelines for this, gender usually plays a role. Some studies say that girls become interested sooner than boys, and may even potty train faster than boys.

To get a better gauge on your own child's level of readiness, you can start by pondering the following questions: does he need assistance getting up onto the toilet? Can he tell you when it's time to go? Has he developed bowel and bladder control? Can he pull off his underwear on his own? Hopefully, you start to get a sense for where he stands.

If you try to potty train a child who isn't ready, the process will likely take a longer time than necessary, thus causing more stress and frustration. It's one thing for you to be ready; it's a whole other thing for your child to be ready. That is the crucial factor that will make your work as a parent SO much easier.

Regardless, the process will demand planning, patience, and your full attention. You'll still have everything else in life going on, which will constantly be threatening to throw your routine off track. If you already know that the coming days or weeks are going to be more chaotic than usual, then you may just want to wait a little longer to begin.

What You'll Need

Let's talk about having the proper equipment. This is an important part of preparation, and will go a long way toward ensuring a smoother process.

In reality, you may not get all the supplies listed below, and probably not all at once. It's best to focus on getting the basics and then move up from there. Here are some of the supplies you'll need. As you read through the list, consider your budget, your personal preferences, your child's preferences, as well as the space that's available in your home.

Toilet Seat

Toilet seats usually vary in size, material, color, and structure. Some come with steps that allow your child to get up easily, or a place where they can rest their feet. Others have latches which allow them to be fixed to the adult toilet. The advantage of these is that you can easily flush waste down the toilet, as well as the fact that your child becomes accustomed to using the big toilet, which can make things easier down the road.

Potty Chairs

There are numerous choices for potty chairs as well. They vary in size, color, and shape. Some do not have a lid, while others do. A few of them also require manual emptying, while others come with a flush.

The primary thing to consider is that your child's feet are stable on the ground, making it easier for them to get up or sit down. The major disadvantage that comes with potty chairs is that they need to be cleaned after each use. And, they eat up a lot of space, which can make things tricky if you have a smaller bathroom.

Step Stool

This is useful for your toddler to easily reach bathroom sinks and toilet seats. Getting more than one will help prevent excessive moving around from place to place. Usually, a single-step stool will do for reaching the toilet. However, a multi-step stool may be required when your child needs to reach the bathroom sink.

Underwear

You'll want to buy underwear for your child before starting. The transition will be easier if you find something in their favorite colors or characters. You can even take him shopping and allow him to choose. This will make the experience more fun. Note – make sure that they fit well so that they come on and off without your help.

Faucet Extenders

Chances are good that it will be difficult for your child to reach the bathroom sink – even with the help of a step stool. With a faucet extender, you can easily extend the reach of your faucet, making it easier for your child to reach and get close to the sink without performing a wild balancing act.

You may consider getting faucet extenders that have attractive colors. You can attach them to all the bathroom sinks that your child will most likely use. Caution – even though you are encouraging your child to use the sink on her own, you will still want to supervise her to make sure that the water temperature she chooses is not too hot.

Training Pants

One thing you'll have to accept in advance is that "accidents" can (and will) occur. Training pants will go a long way toward making mishaps less messy. Training pants are types of underwear that have padding attached at their center and between the legs to absorb leaks. They help because when such accidents happen, your child gets to feel wet and soiled. It will give him a not-so-pleasant feeling that he will want to avoid. Another benefit is that they can be reused and are affordable.

Loose Clothing

Another essential supply is loose-fitting clothes. Having tight garments will make it harder for him to take off pants and pull them back on. It may also cause more accidents, because of how they restrict movement. Complicated dresses and rompers with multiple buttons and fasteners are not the best choices. Sweatpants, loose shorts, or dresses will work better. You may also want to consider clothes that are easy to wash.

Waterproof Mattress Cover

One of the most challenging tasks to face is having to clean up a soiled mattress. One way to prevent this is by getting a protective cover for the bed. Materials usually vary, as some may be vinyl while others may have a waterproof lower layer and a cotton upper layer. It is advisable to have more than a single mattress cover to help manage accidents.

Cleaning Equipment

The best way to prepare for mishaps is to equip yourself with supplies that make cleaning easier and less messy. Therefore, having a stock of rags or paper towels, sanitizers, and disinfectants will help.

Potty Timer

An essential thing to incorporate into your child's potty training is regular potty breaks. This will help her get accustomed to the whole process, hence reducing the accidents that occur. Having a potty timer that goes off every 30 minutes will serve as a reminder for your child to go potty.

Progress Chart

A brilliant way to show your toddler that she is on track and making good progress is by helping her draw her progress chart. This will make visiting the toilet fun for her.

Choosing the Right Potty

Picking a potty for your child can be one of the most mentally taxing jobs of all. This is because there are an overwhelming number of options to choose from. And, a thousand and one factors you're trying to sort out as you decide.

There are two primary types of potties: the seat reducer and the stand-alone potty. You need to think of simplicity, safety, space, and size. Your child must be able to find the potty chair comfortable and easy enough to get on any time. Try to select the best fit for your kid.

There are many rim sizes too. You do not want to get one that will leave your child feeling unsure. Getting a potty that is too big or too small for your child's bottom will probably hamper the experience, so do your due diligence in finding the right one.

If you have a boy, then you may want to consider getting a splash guard. This tool will help limit the mess (and cleanup) after use. It shouldn't be placed s high that he can't reach it, but it also shouldn't be so low that he misses his target.

Another factor that you should consider is cleanup. Getting a seat reducer will mean that it is already attached to your regular toilet seat. Hence, it won't need any major cleaning as you can flush the feces or urine down the toilet. On the other hand, getting a stand-alone potty entails that you will have some cleaning work every time.

Potty seats also differ when it comes to rim shape. Some may be square-shaped, while the majority of potty rim seats are round. Round-shaped potty seats are preferred, as they do a better job of ensuring that your child is securely seated.

As mentioned, involving your child in the selection process will build excitement and anticipation in him. It will serve as a confidence booster for him as well, as it reminds him that he played a role in the process.

Clearing Your Schedule

In a successful potty training regiment, the majority of the job is carried out by the parent. Yet it is not as straightforward as just switching your child's diapers to underwear and waiting for them to let you know when they're ready.

The truth is that starting potty training is not easy, and it may even feel as though you're the one being trained. It will demand your time, mind, and a lot of resources. For this reason, it is best to clear your calendar as best as possible. The whole reason you need to potty train is because you are unable to schedule your child's bathroom use, so you need to make yourself more available than usual. Taking on extra tasks during this time probably isn't wise. You'll want a stable schedule, and you'll want to be home all day.

At the start, be careful not to be too forceful. Every child is different. While it may take one child just two days to get the hang of potty training, another child may need more time. Give him time – away from distractions. And, try to stay in one location so that you have home court advantage, and familiarity working on your side. Do your best to avoid using bathrooms in new locations, as this may leave your child confused.

Potty training will require you to have a timer. Start by setting the timer to 20-minute intervals and then gradually increase that amount of time. You can eventually move on to 30-minutes, 45-minutes, or an hour. Eventually, you won't even need a timer. At the start, however, it will help keep you consistent.

One of the main reasons your child has accidents is because she isn't paying attention to the urges in her body. Another reason is because you forget potty breaks. Your job is to take her to the potty, no matter how much fun she is having. The truth is that she probably won't need to go to the bathroom every 20 minutes. However, this interval will allow her time to get familiar with the potty and the process. You will have fewer accidents. It is vital to note that if your child can't stay dry and is always soiled within 10 to 15-minute intervals, it may be an indication that she isn't quite ready yet. You may want to wait a few weeks months before giving it another try.

What You Can Expect

The primary cause of frustration when potty is high expectations coupled with slow progress. As a parent, you must always be wary of comparing your child with other people's children. There is no need to compare. It can lead to a lot of frustration and negative emotions. Understand that just because your child shows interest in potty, doesn't mean it will be smooth sailing. Potty training requires patience and understanding; it's a process. It demands practice. All the aspects of potty training have to be mastered by your child, and this will take time to learn. You need to train him on how to detect his toilet-related urges and respond to them appropriately. It's a whole new concept to your him. Therefore, it will take a while to master. Attempting to rush him will only leave him feeling bad and you feeling stressed.

Take time to examine what matters to you. Are you more concerned with getting speedy results, or with the happiness and confidence of your child? The fact is that she can sense when you're frustrated, and your not-so-covert frustration may only be met with more resistance. Expect that she will make mistakes. Accidents are bound to occur along the way.

The best way to view this process is to compare it with your child speaking her first words or taking her first step; it happens at the right time – never sooner. When you begin to see it this way, you will come to realize that she needs your support and love more than anything else. There is no need to make potty training all about yourself—because it's not. Potty training is about her, and her needs come first.

There are so many outside forces that can feed your frustrations. The cost of diapers, the inconvenience of frequent diaper changes, or the stuff that all of your friends are saying. All these factors make you feel and expect too much. Instead of assuming that your child will get the hang of potty training within the first two hours, choose to focus on your potty training schedule. This will keep your mind occupied with the right things, rather than keep you stressed and feeling out of control.

It Won't Go Perfectly

While you can expect frustrations, be encouraged that it will get better. The process of learning is always loaded with mistakes, and potty training is no exception. Your child may even regress in the process. She may forget the skills that you have initially taught her. It's normal to feel upset when she keeps making the same mistakes over and over – especially after you feel you've already trained her effectively. Don't worry. It's a natural response. Instead of nagging and making her feel pressured to please you, give her encouraging smiles that show you support her – no matter what stage she is in.

You can expect to feel stressed and fatigued, and so will your child. Even the most trivial things will affect her progress. Family conflicts or routine changes, such as switching daycare centers, can affect how she responds. Be sensitive to her response. Be careful not to overreact. Don't let the stress cause you to punish, scold, or criticize her. But, if you happen to make a mistake, accept it. Forgive yourself. Don't compound the negativity.

Apologize to your child and resolve to do better in the future.

Part of preparation involves knowing that there are some things you can't prepare for. At best, you can prepare to be surprised. Here are some of the challenges that you'll probably face as you explore the world of potty training:

Your child ALWAYS relying on you to get to the potty.

Your child may not be able (or willing) to get to the potty on his own. It will take a while for him to recognize and respond on time to his body's urges. You can help him by letting him know how proud of him you are and how big you think he is. You can make him see that he doesn't need your help to get to the potty. He can do it on his own! With some patience, he'll eventually get it.

Not wanting to get onto the potty at all

You can combat this issue by mentally preparing your child. You have to assess your child correctly, and that is why he needs your full attention. If he refuses to get on the potty, have a conversation with him and ask him why. Reassure his doubts and help build his confidence on the matter.

If you find that a heart-to-heart talk doesn't help, you can always use the reward system. Buy a cool toy that you know he likes, and keep it somewhere where he can see it. When he asks for it (which he will… continuously), tell him that he can only have it if he sits on the potty 3 to 5 times – whatever you think is a good number. This will provide him incentive that he otherwise wouldn't have.

Only wanting to make use of the potty when at home

It is normal for kids to get attached to things – even small things, such as a certain breakfast bowl or a toothbrush. It can also be the case that your child may feel attached to a particular potty seat or toilet. This can make things difficult if you happen to be on the go.

One way you can solve this is by bringing a portable potty or potty seat along when you know you'll be away. This is another place where a conversation might help. You can mentally prep your child for those times when you know he will be entering new territory. Let him know that the difference in environment is okay. Try to make him feel less insecure.

Having frequent accidents at night

Successful training during the day may not carry into the night. The truth is that most potty training accidents happen at night. This is when they are less guarded, and you are not able to practice your usual 30-minute potty breaks. This does not mean that you can't have potty breaks at night, but you they shouldn't be as frequent. Two potty breaks a night should probably be enough. Going beyond two may be excessive, as well as disruptive for you and you're child's sleep. You may also choose to make use of disposable training pants, as this will make any messes more manageable.

As a parent, a large part of your job is to provide security. Don't sound discouraged and never let doubts overwhelm you. The truth is that your child *is* getting better, and this should stay at the forefront of your mind. It won't always go perfectly, but your attitude will largely determine how the journey will go.

Final thoughts

Again, the main person who needs to prepare for potty training is you. It can be unnerving to think of the stress involved. It will require you to be emotionally, financially, and physically prepared. It will be demanding, and you'll want to be sure that you've covered all your bases.

If you happen to love order, structure, and cleanliness, there will be a bit of sacrifice involved. Because, as Mick Jagger once stated, "You can't always get what you want." This will be one of those times.

You'll need more than mere intuition; you must have a method, or well-sketched plan. It will give you consistency, and ensure your child's success. It will also make your job as a parent much easier, giving you peace of mind whenever doubts and questions arise. You'll be less likely to underestimate or overestimate the challenges.

If you've potty trained before, don't rely too heavily on the methods that have worked for you in the past; make a new plan that you know will be best suited for your child, because every child is different, and so is every life season. Take into consideration how your life may have changed since the last time. Take into consideration any unique situations that your life may currently present.

Potty training boys is different than potty training girls, and vice versa. Potty training twins or special needs children will also require more than your old rulebook can provide. Potty training as a single parent is different than potty training with a partner, and vice versa. Potty training as a secretary may be different from potty-training as a firefighter, which could require you to be on call at all hours. Tailor your own unique routine to your current life situation. That will ensure the best possible outcome.

And, it can't be said enough that no one is perfect. You and your child are going to make mistakes. Allow enough grace for the both of you. Be sure that you aren't transferring stress or frustration from any other areas of life. As much as it is about practical matters, it is about mindset and emotions. Your attitude will be the backbone that keeps the process in line.

Keep that old "This too shall pass" mantra playing in your mind. Do what you must to stay balanced. Yoga. A spin class. Jimmy Buffet and some sangria (but not too much). Talk to a friend who's been there, and share a laugh. Stay well rested. Don't neglect your own needs for water and nourishing food. The ride may be overwhelming, but it's necessary, and it will take you to a better place.

Chapter 2: Other Preparation

Changing Your Lingo

Ever wonder why the primary ways that children learn are with songs and colorful pictures? It's because these things get them excited, and their excitement leads to learning. In short, this is why language will play a vital role in how quickly your child catches on.

Many parents get confused about the language they should use. They wonder if it's okay to use words like feces, urine, or bowel movements. They wonder if they should restrict their mode of communication to basic terms like poo or pee.

On one hand, using straightforward, biological language helps set a matter-of-fact tone. There isn't anything bad about using the potty, so we don't have to sugar-coat our language to describe it. It's a normal biological process, so it is fitting to use factual, anatomically correct, and scientifically accurate wording. Similarly, there isn't anything necessarily funny about our bodily functions, so there is no need for funny-sounding or made-up speech. This perspective may help in the long run because it sets a strong foundation for another important conversation down the road — sex. Establishing a baseline here of scientific language for body parts and processes should form a precedent for speaking about the facts of human sexuality.

Although there is nothing wrong or inappropriate with either style, it's good to consider the pros and cons of each in your approach. Make sure that your language reflects you — your values and your preferred parenting style. And, think of the impact. The benefit of using words that sound cute is that they might make your child more interested in learning. Referring to a penis as a "wee-wee" may even get a giggle out of *you*.

Giving your child fun words — or better yet, having her create them, could make her feel freer and more confident about the whole process. You're giving her a free ticket to practice self-expression. Perhaps the only real rule here is that you use common sense. Don't use words that leave your child feeling ashamed for wanting to go, or words that you think are inappropriate. The fact is that your child notices when a word doesn't feel right to you, or when you say things that you normally correct others for saying.

If you're running low on ideas, you might consider incorporating words and language that your child's preschool makes use of frequently. This can add yet another layer of familiarity. Then again, you may happen to discover that you don't really appreciate the words that they use. In which case, you have a good opportunity to let them know your opinion and ask them to change the words that they expose your child to daily.

Using fun or made-up words has its advantages – especially when your child has issues with his command of language. The language you choose should make him feel comfortable and safe about every aspect of potty training. If your spouse uses words that you feel are inappropriate, then this is something that you both should sort out. You shouldn't let your potty training language be controversial – in the household or among any other third parties. The truth is that your child will most likely use these same words at any time and in any setting. Grocery store checkout? "Dookie!" Church service? "My penis has to let the tinkles out!" Think about the different settings you'll be in, as well as the different people who will be listening.

Mental Preparation

Potty training your child is like exposing her to a brand new world. She'll do better if she can feel excited about it, so you'll have to let her know what lies ahead. Many children love copying the acts of others and doing what they see their older siblings or parents do. They love to play the role of an adult; it makes them feel confident. You can definitely use this to your advantage.

An excellent way to let him ease into potty training is by setting the stage for him. You can have a pre-rehearsal for the whole process. You can show him around the bathroom and explain in a fun way what happens in there. You can show him how to take off his underwear and even allow him to sit on the toilet seat for a while. Teach him how to use the bathroom sink or toilet paper. Let him see how fun flushing can be and the benefits of handwashing. Be creative, and you're bound to think of ways to get your child to imitate you.

Children are always interested in explanations and learning how processes work. The critical thing here is to make this as fun as possible. Try to be carefree. Let your child feel free to ask questions and express herself. You can also explain why she needs to be potty trained and all the related benefits. Talk about her body and the importance of expelling waste. Let her see that it's nothing to be shy about. Let her feel proud and secure about going potty. You can use pets as an example if you have any. Show her that her pet has to go potty too, just like her.

If possible, try to make use of illustrations. You can use her favorite doll to show her how sitting on the potty seat will be like. Let her see that it's nothing to be scared about, and let her feel like she is not alone. This kind of practice may seem silly, but it actually helps your child understand the process in a way that easily relates to her. This kind of mental preparation will make the ride a whole lot easier for both of you. And, having her full cooperation (and excitement) will help a great deal.

Other Products That Help

The good thing about potty training is that you don't need to face the battle on your own. There are now so many products and tools that make life SO MUCH easier for you and your child. They will help you do a better job of training and assist you with the work. Some of these products include:

Potty Training Doll

These serve as a model for your child. They act as a visual learning tool. You simply fill them up with water from your kitchen faucet, and then, a short time later, that water needs to come out. You then help your child put the toy on its potty seat, and it starts to pee. This helps your child understand that eating and drinking leads to going potty. It helps you easily convey the mechanics of what's happening, and do so in a way that your child will easily comprehend.

Toilet Targets

This product is specifically for males. It's basically a target that you place in the toilet, which he can try to aim for. They are fun supplies that make potty training more enjoyable. You can place several of them in different areas within the toilet and tell your child to aim for them. It makes urinating fun and exciting – just like playing a game. And let's be honest – plenty of grown-up men would enjoy this too. Maybe a nice Christmas gift for your husband?

Potty Training Books

Another trick worth having up your sleeve is to use potty training as a story time for your child. Not only will this be entertaining, it can also teach the basics about potty training in a way that helps your child learn faster and more efficiently. There are many potty training books available in the market today. It will help your child feel better if he sees that his favorite characters had to learn to use the potty too. Listening to stories is an excellent way to teach your child in a way that he enjoys. These books are full of hilarious illustrations and playful texts that will help your child feel more familiar with the concept of potty training. Remember, it is all about making the journey easier for your little learner.

Pants with Stretchy Waistband

An excellent way to encourage your child to take off her pants on her own is by providing pants that are easy to remove. Pants with many buttons and zippers will probably be difficult to take off. Spend the money necessary to get pants that have a stretchy waistband. Let such attire form the bulk of your child's clothes during potty training. This way, there will be less chance of accidents. Plus, they are easy to find and will be comfortable for your child.

Rewards

Here's another great way to make sure your child succeeds. We call it "a reward system," because, well… that sounds better than saying bribery. Regardless of what you call it, it's an extremely effective way to motivate your little champ and make him excited about the journey. Remember the cool toy idea we talked about? Well, that's the gist of it. Give him something he wants for doing it right. Praise is nice, but so is a brand new Spiderman figure. This is an okay time to spoil your child a little. In the end, it will make both of your lives easier.

Chapter 3: Starting

Bye-Bye Diapers

Convincing your child to graduate out of diapers is one of the most significant challenges you'll face. After all, who wouldn't prefer the option of being able to pee and multitask simultaneously (No need for a show of hands)?

An excellent way to help your child recognize the benefits of a diaper-free lifestyle is to incorporate training pants into your routine. They will help him understand the relationship between the needs of his body and the need for the potty chair. Many children hate the sensation of feeling wet and soiled, and training pants enable them to experience that discomfort as a motivator. It's one thing to let your child know that he will get damp and uncomfortable when he doesn't do his business in the potty; it's another thing to let him experience it for himself. He will soon quickly prefer the comfort that comes with being dry – achieved only by making it to the potty in time.

One important factor that can delay transition is the continued presence of diapers in your child's environment.

Having them in plain sight can give your child the wrong impression – that you **aren't** serious about potty training. He might get mixed messages, and feel that he still has a choice between using the potty and using those familiar diapers that once provided so much freedom. If your child can easily see and handle diapers, then he is probably going to keep asking for them. So it is best to put them out of sight.

If you find it hard to get rid of the diapers in your house, you may want to have an honest conversation with yourself. Ask yourself why you can't seem to let them go. Are you sentimental? Or, maybe you see them as an easy way out of the stress you are currently feeling.

One of the main barriers of moving forward is holding on too tightly to the past. Understand that your child is growing, and this progress is necessary. It's the natural progress of your child's life. Though it may be difficult, try to accept it and even embrace it.

Going All the Way

Children excel within a carefully planned routine in the hands of a diligent teacher who knows what she is doing. They tend not to respond well to surprises and changes in their routine. They also tend not to flourish as well in a disorganized setting. Therefore, your job is to make their transition as organized and predictable as possible. It starts with **you** getting all you need for potty training. Your **FULL** preparation and pace are fundamental to their success.

When you start right, your child will be able to sense that you've gotten your ducks in a row. You will be relaxed and happy. It will show in your voice and your overall disposition. They will feel confident enough to trust you for the guidance and encouragement that they need.

Here are some miscellaneous tips that should help:

- Tell your child to pull her underwear COMPLETELY off so that she can go quickly when she sits down.

- Show her how to place her elbows on her knees and shift her body forward, as this helps her relax her pelvic muscles better.

- Teach her to sit in such a way that her bottom is directly in the toilet opening.

These tips may seem obvious, but you probably wouldn't believe how many people either don't think to do them, or forget. Such basic things will speak to your child's fears and doubts and even influence your own confidence as a trainer. Another tip is to consider placing a nighttime potty chair next to your child's bed so that he can pee at night will. Also, you may want to make sure **all** bathrooms are set up. Some families pick a single bathroom in the house. You can go around the house and make sure that EACH bathroom is prepared well (and not too overstimulating). As much as possible, take away unnecessary items from the toilet area. For example, you can remove all trash cans, cleaning items, or clothing hampers to allow for more room and eliminate distractions.

The Importance of Drinking Water

A frequent intake of fluids serves to quickly bring your child's bladder to full capacity – an excellent way of helping her master and understand the feeling of having to go. This will help her develop bladder control. It will also decrease her chances of developing urinary tract infections and constipation, since dehydration has a direct link to bowel and bladder problems. You build your child's habits early; as time passes, they become well-incorporated into her daily routine.

It's best to get this programmed into them at a young age. Children have body processes that promote thirst due to their increased activity levels and fluid loss rates. They also get dehydrated easily because their excretion system is not yet well-developed. Therefore, it is essential to let your child drink a lot of water.

Using the toilet can be difficult for your child when he is constipated. It can cause pain and discomfort. Ensuring a steady fluid intake will also give him more chances to use the potty. It will help him understand the urge to urinate and let him see the right response for the feeling.

Reinforce New Habits As Consistently As Possible

It's hard to overstate the importance of repetition, as it plays such a vital role in transmitting necessary information to your child's subconscious mind. It is by repetition that your child can correctly identify colors, names, the letters of the alphabet, and even your face.

The more you repeat information, the more he will retain. Spaced reinforcement (offering information, allowing time for its application, and then repeating the information) is a learning method that serves to ensure that a fundamental aspect of knowledge sticks. Since most things are new to young children, it's better to err on the side of saying things too often than saying things too infrequently.

You should constantly be informing them of the most essential habits, such as pulling off their clothes, sitting on the potty, wiping their bottom, and washing their hands well. If your child struggles to put into action the things that you have told her countless times, it doesn't mean that she is unintelligent; it means she is still developing the ability to learn. Repetition helps her to give particular attention to what is important and necessary. It also shows that you are serious about the issue and that it is solid enough for her to stand on, without exceptions. It might seem like it's not working at times, but do not lose heart. Sometimes, simpler is better. Just because this technique doesn't seem too sophisticated doesn't mean it's ineffective. With ample time, your efforts will produce results. Your child is more likely to master concepts that she has seen you demonstrate multiple times and heard you talk about over and over again.

Celebrate Every Success

One vital thing that you must never lose sight of is praising your child. As he makes progress and has fewer accidents, you must always stop and give credit to the efforts he is making. Celebrating his success doesn't have to be a massive event; it can simply be clapping, an encouraging word, or a smile. Doing this will help your child better understand that you value his efforts. It will also train you to be an encouraging person to him throughout all seasons of life.

Celebrations should become a ritual, forming the bulk of your responses. This will have both short-term and long-term effects on your child, as you are instilling in him the habit of focusing on the good. It is a mindset that will transfer into how he views and experience the world. It will also make him feel more confident about himself, and about the role you play in his life.

Get Others Involved

Chances are good that your child has a strong desire to gain the approval of those around her. This forms one of the most important tools that a parent can have in his/her arsenal – approval and acceptance of behavior that is desirable. Of course, getting other people involved can greatly add to this effect.

Try to communicate your intentions with those who have direct and regular contact with your child. This list will include: older siblings, aunts, uncles, in-laws, caregivers, and even neighbors. Your child needs all the support and help that she can get, and it will help if everyone who is involved is on the same page.

You will also have to let them in on the little details such as the potty language you use for your child. Inform them if your child is frightened or anxious about any aspect of potty training. Tell them about the signs that your child displays when it's time to go, how she reacts when she has an accident, and which responses from others she is embarrassed by. Making them aware of such information will not only assist your child in getting more comfortable, it will also reduce the burden that you bear. Plus, your child will transition more quickly. Involving others will also leave room for you to learn new techniques and methods to add to your current strategy.

Naps and Bedtime

A common issue that parents face is the uncertainty of knowing how to handle naps and bedtimes. Daytime potty training demands that your child be socially, physiologically, and emotionally prepared. For best results, he should also have well-developed communication skills. He is going through a lot during the day already, and having to use the potty can disrupt his regular routine. Having to wake him up at night can serve as the last straw that "breaks the camel's back."

During potty training, you must ensure your child is as well-rested as possible. A tired kid is a cranky student, and this will only slow down the learning process. Since it is so important for your child to have good sleep during this time, many experienced pediatricians believe that using diapers for bedtimes during the initial periods of potty training may not be a horrible idea. However, you must be sure to let your child know that the diapers are ONLY for night time. You may even want to give them a different name. Rather than calling them diapers, call them "pull-ups" or "Night time pants." Assure him that they will come off the moment he is awake. Ensure that he uses the potty minutes before bed time (or nap time). This will help him become conscious of what he needs to do to remain dry. It will also build a regular habit.

Daytime naps are a good practice for how you (and your child) will handle night time. As time goes by, you can try switching to training pants and underwear so that he gets to feel when he is wet. This will help your child sense the need to go – even when sleeping.

Here are some points that will help you handle naps and nighttimes:

- Don't put pressure on your child. Offer praises when she stays dry throughout the night. If she doesn't, try not to see it as too big of a concern.

- In the event that your child wakes up during the night, encourage her to use the potty before you tuck her back into bed.

- Understand that night time training may take a longer time to master. Let most of your attention rest on her training in the daytime.

- Make nighttimes as comfortable as possible. For example, if your child is scared of going into a dark bathroom at night, keep the bathroom and hallway well-lit for her. Also, making the toilet accessible will limit accidents as much as possible. Keeping the bathroom door open will also help.

- Ensure that your child understands that she shouldn't be timid about waking you up at night if she feels the need to go. Let her know that she has your support no matter what, both day and night.

Staying The Course

It's normal to feel overwhelmed during this process. Sometimes you may even feel as though you are right back where you started, without much progress to show for your efforts. During such times, you must understand that your child is getting better and that you are getting more experienced. There are many potty training problems that may arise as you continue on the journey, but the solution is to stick to the training and to resist the urge to go back to using diapers.

Here are some tips that will help:

Embrace the tough times

Have an important conversation with yourself — one where you admit the true difficulties of what you're facing. Reassure yourself that change doesn't always come easy. Acknowledge that there will be TONS of booboos, but you'll deal with them.

Never see mistakes as a failure

Sometimes progress isn't visible. Improvements are often subtle and hard to detect. It'll often be one step forward, two steps backward. However, the overall trend is still gradually going upward. Try not to tally up mistakes. You will drive yourself crazy. Instead, remain focused on the bigger picture.

Be a realist

By now, we've hopefully given you a pretty fair picture of the challenges you will be facing. If so, that's good. We're trying to burst any bubbles you may have about perfection.

One thing that will keep you sane is to have realistic expectations. That way, you're less likely to feel discouraged by slow progress.

Go easy… on yourself

Self-criticism is a major barrier to staying on track. Keep in mind that just as you must give patience and encouragement to your child, you should do the same to yourself. Recognize that what you're doing isn't easy, and try not to be hard on yourself when life happens. Because, it probably will.

Set your priorities

There are many issues that your child may experience when potty training. He probably hasn't learned to wipe yet. He may not know how to wash his hands, or may even wet himself at night. Whatever the issue, ensure that you are focused on what matters most – teaching him the core skill of using the potty. One goal at a time. You can worry about other things once you've gotten the main trick mastered.

Dos and Don'ts

Potty training your child can be a sensitive task. There are many things that you should and shouldn't do. Here are some dos and don'ts that will improve your chances of success.

Potty Training Dos
Stop comparing

One of the primary causes of failure is comparing your child to other children. Your friend tells you about her 2 day success story, and suddenly you feel pressured to match her. But, if you focus to much on what other people say, you will be less focused on the realistic needs of your child. Don't make the mistake of keeping up with the Jones'. Chances are, they're embellishing their story anyway.

Keep a daily log

One thing you can do to lessen accidents is to write down those times when your child uses the potty. This is wise, since there is no official rulebook. Does he seem to go at certain times of day? Right after meals? Right after nap time? Make note of it, and you'll soon begin to see a pattern, and have a reference for future use. Of course, it won't be clockwork; it'll just be a basic tool that helps you reduce the overall number of accidents.

Switch it up

If it seems like a certain approach isn't working for your child, that's okay. You aren't married to it. Make whichever modifications you need to in order to improve the journey. Does she refuse to drink lots of water? Okay, have her drink less. Does she not want to use the upstairs toilet? Okay, use the one downstairs. The point isn't to keep to your regiment; the point is to achieve potty training success!

Clean up with a smile

While you yourself aren't particularly fond of accidents, the truth is that your child feels bad about accidents too. Parents often voice their displeasure, unintentionally shaming their children for how they've fallen short. But, that only produces bad long-term results. Try not to let it show that you're angry or upset when helping with cleanup; instead, let him know that you understand and that you believe he is getting better. Saying words like "I know you'll get it next time" or "Wow! You were so close to the potty" or "You've got this" will help him feel less pressured about making mistakes.

Have an emergency kit

You can't dictate when an accident will occur; that's why it's called an accident. There are chances that your child may feel the need to go when you're away from home. So, plan for those moments by having an extra pairs of underwear, disposable potty seat covers, a change of clothes, and lots of wet wipes. You can add other items if you want to, including your child's favorite toy or book. Having prepared adequately will be a lifesaver at times.

Ask for help when needed

When it comes to children, you don't know everything. Even though you may sometimes feel like you've got it all together, you'll probably still find it handy to have some extra resources at your disposal. This can include your mother, relatives, or friends who've been through the process. If you want professional help, you may want to talk to a nurse or doctor. Pediatricians are experts at dealing with children. In fact, your child should have a pediatrician whom you can quickly seek out in times of need. Don't be ashamed to ask for advice. Asking for help when you need it isn't a sign of weakness, but rather, of strength.

Potty Training Don'ts
Don't give excessive rewards

While it's important to celebrate every success and progress, you don't want to overdo it. Providing small treats and stickers isn't bad. However, when you make it a habit to shower your child with too much sugar and expensive toys, you can easily create new problems.

Keep in mind that rewards can also create pressure, which may cause your child to feel anxious. If she knows that a lot is at stake, she may buckle under the pressure. You may choose to save the bigger rewards for the bigger milestones, and give small rewards for small successes.

Note - you also don't want to relay to your child that your kindness and generosity are conditional. Make sure she feels loved and valued even when she fails. Even when she doesn't get the reward, you can still give your love and encouragement.

Don't punish

This is the other side of the "Don't give excessive rewards" coin. Just as you can do harm by too much lavish, you can also do harm by punishing your child for his accidents. Even though you're stressed about work, you're in a hurry, and now you're cleaning up dirty underwear for the fiftieth time this week, try to remain calm. And, more importantly, do NOT send the message to your child that he has done something wrong.

Often, when we're in such situations, this is a very easy mistake to make. We're used to saying no to our children. We're used to reprimanding them for spilling their milk. It may be very natural for us to shoot a stern look without even thinking about it, or instinctively raise our voices. Bear in mind that children are very sensitive to our reactions. Try to keep them governed, or you'll end up creating a sense of fear in them that they associate with going potty.

Don't stop halfway

Life is the excuse that we all have, and which we all constantly use. But, remember that in this journey, consistency is crucial. If you've started, stay the course. Don't take a day off and go back to the plan later. This will send confusing messages to your child, and it will also cause the process to take longer. Plus, you'll find yourself having to re-teach a lot of the same lessons, which will feel tedious and draining.

Don't give in to tantrums or schmoozing.

There are two primary ways that children try to get what they want – throwing a fit, and being extra nice. If you're not strong (and if you don't recognize what's happening), they'll play you like a Steinway piano. You need to be firm in your potty training guidance, not giving into your child's attempts to sway you. If they are upset about having to go to the potty, that's okay. They'll get over it. In the meantime, stand your ground in a kind way. Calmly explain to them why they need to use the potty, and tell them that it's time.

Also, be careful about giving time-outs when your child throws a tantrum – that may be just what they're hoping for! A time-out means time away from doing what they don't want to do.

Don't be overly controlling

While it's true that you will sometimes have to take charge, you also don't want to become too controlling. This is another common mistake we can make. It can quickly suck all the joy out of learning for your child if she feels you're trying too hard to "pound in the knowledge."

As you fight to remain strong, also try to trust – that your own approach is working, and that your child will eventually get it. Also, remember your other options:

encouragement and rewards. Continue to use the other tools that we've talked about so far, such as books or a potty doll. These are things that your child understands, and they'll re-motivate her when she needs new incentive.

Don't wait for a request

Potty training is your job, which means you make the plan. You can't rely on your child to ask you if he can now go to the potty. You'll have to stay ahead of his urges to go, because he isn't yet accustomed to using the potty, and because he might be too shy (or wait too long) to ask. Remember to use the timer. Remember to have him drink fluids.

Don't set a deadline

While it's true that it's possible to successfully potty train your child in just three days (and while it's also true that following the advice in this book should get you there), you should also be careful not to mandate that it happens in that amount of time. It may happen sooner. It may take a little longer. Three days is a goal; not a deadline. If you're halfway through day three and feeling as though your child is nowhere close to being ready, that's okay. Keep going.

This is also why you may want to give yourself a little more time than necessary. Because, even if things go exactly as planned, you're still not finished. There are still things you'll have to keep doing in order to help your child retain the knowledge and skills she has learned. That, we will talk about next!

Chapter 4: Afterwards
So, It's Over... right?

Congratulations. You've managed to help your child graduate to big kid pants! Do the curtains come up now? Not really. You still have your work cut out for you. There are a few things you should know:

At first, you will probably live with a bit of fear. You will wonder if the training will "stick." You may even try to get your child to go even when he doesn't don't need to. And why wouldn't you? You've been traumatized in the past by your share of surprises.

Not that you shouldn't be careful; it's just that you are in a new stage. It may take you some time to truly realize (and believe) that. And, it doesn't hurt to continue erring on the side of caution. After all, just because you've graduated, doesn't mean there's no need for caution.

Sometimes, you'll hear your child telling you that she needs to go potty. You'll drive to the nearest Starbucks, dash in, wipe down the toilet seat, and wait for your child to go. Then... nothing. Just a silly smile that says, "False alarm."

Keep in mind that you should still pack extra clothes when you go out – just in case there are any messes. Heaven forbid you are out in public for an entire day without any extra clothes when your child suddenly has an accident. It could be a really long and stinky adventure.

Know that wherever you go, you may need to rush to the closest bathroom. Try to have an emergency strategy in mind in case you need to make that mad dash! Also, consider the type of toilet that you'll be using if you go. Some kids are afraid of motion-sensor flushing. You might create a panic attack if they're sitting on the potty and it flushes by itself.

You also want to keep in mind that some places just don't have nice toilets – you don't want your child to end up sitting on a giant, filthy thing that who knows what has been splashed on, and who knows when it was last cleaned. Yuck!

Remember also that you should:

Continue To Reinforce Good Behavior

As we've discussed, children love to hear their parents mentioning how well they are doing. They need it. During potty training, and even after. That's right – you should still continue to do this – even once your child seems to have gotten the hang of things.

You could cause your child some confusion if you were to suddenly stop doing all those things you did during potty training. It may feel strange and unnatural, and may even make him wonder if he has done something wrong. After all, he's made an association between your good words and his good efforts. Keep that association alive!

Let your praise be as honest, sincere, and simple as possible

Your praises should aim to encourage the right behavior. Your words should keep him motivated and improve his self-esteem. If your child doesn't think you are sincere, then any positive effects are lost. Manipulative praise may also have the same effects. Children usually have a sense for when you are merely trying to coerce them. For these reasons, ensure that your praise is as sincere and honest as possible.

Don't direct your praises to their ability

Some parents only praise their kids when they win first place. The message they send is, "I'm proud of you… because you won!" Instead, try to direct your praises to your child's efforts; not his abilities. You're not proud of him for what he is capable of. At least, not as much as you're proud of him for how hard he tries! You want him to know that even if he fails in life, you'll still be proud – provided that he gave his effort.

Be specific

Children respond to praise better when they know exactly why they're getting it. Abstract praises don't tell them what they did right. The more descriptive the praise, the more your child will understand it. And, the more likely she will see it as sincere. Making your praise as descriptive as possible makes her see that you notice her efforts and are dutifully paying attention to what she is doing right. You can aim to say, "I love how you took off your pants so fast and ran to the potty," rather than a vague "That's great."

Don't offer comparison praise

Giving praise that compares your child with others is sure to backfire. This will cause her to believe that she is competing with other children, thus making her feel like the goal is to win, rather than learn. If ever she finds it hard to master tasks like wiping or flushing the toilet, she may feel like a loser.

Don't offer praise that is conditional

We've talked a little about conditional praise, which usually has a single intent: to control. When you give praise to your child about something, you don't want his first thought to be, "Oh great. I wonder what she wants me to do this time." Praise shouldn't be solely about getting results. It should be an opportunity for you to speak positive truths from your heart. You don't want your child to feel as though his worth depends on your validation. So, continue to give validation – even when your hopes and expectations aren't met.

Try not to praise excessively

Children may feel that when you praise them too often or too outlandishly that you have low expectations of them. Or, it can make them feel that they are entitled to recognition for every little task they perform. You don't want that to be their only motivation. You want them to do their best because of the inherent value of whichever achievement they are giving their efforts to.

Further, excessive praise can make your child feel overwhelmed and pressured not to have accidents. He may feel scared and may even become depressed when he makes a mistake.

Many people refer to praise as a double-edged tool. When offered the right way, it can lead to beautiful results and act as a motivation. When offered the wrong way, it can cause suspicion, resistance, and feelings of low self-worth.

There's Still No Such Thing As Perfection

Remember that life is… well, life. When has it ever gone just as planned? You cover all of your bases trying to get dinner ready in time, and then nobody shows up when it's ready, and everyone ends up heating it up in the microwave. Making the switch from diapers to underwear will be similar. Some days, it'll go just as you planned. You'll be sailing along smoothly without a single complication. The next day, you'll find yourself wondering if potty your training lessons ever even happened, and you'll wonder which planet you're on.

Here are some common frustrations and problems you're bound to face after potty training:

Your child thinks he should play with his poop

Think about it for a moment from a toddler's perspective… This substance that comes out of his rear end is actually pretty amazing. It is often malleable and moldable. Sometimes it even comes out already molded into pretty fascinating shapes. Other times it's softer and is the right consistency for finger painting. Sometimes it floats. Sometimes it sinks. It can have a range of colors. And the smell, though disgusting for those of us conditioned to dislike it, is fabulously rich and unique.

Consider also that throughout his first years of life, a child's experience with poop has been to watch his parent or caregiver use their hands to scoop it up, wipe it up, and carry it away. With all of these factors in play, why wouldn't a youngster without a lifetime of reference points for proper behavior want to play with his poop?

If your kid is trying to play with his poop, you should know that this behavior is due to his curiosity. When he was in diapers, he didn't get to see it and examine it, so it might seem new to him to get to see his feces. The key here is to inform him, gently but seriously, that he mustn't play with his poop. It will help to give this instruction in a clear and calm voice.

Your child makes a fuss when you flush his poop away

Kids may feel offended to watch you flush their waste away because they see their waste as a part of themselves. Again, this is an example of a parent's role in educating the child about reality. The poop is not meant to be a part of him. That's why it has been pushed out of the body. You can try to avoid your child's distress by explaining to them the basic needs of the body to produce and eliminate waste products.

Your child has accidents moments after being taken off the potty

This is a common problem that usually occurs at the early stages of potty training. The cause of this issue is because your child is just getting familiar with relaxing the muscles that are associated with bladder and bowel control. This concern is best solved with patience, calmness, and persistence.

Your child only wants to use the potty when a specific person is around

This happens in a lot of cases. The key is for that person to invite another person along and then gradually withdraw himself and allow others to help your child on the potty.

Your child only recognizes the need to poop but not the need to pee

Most children respond to bowel movements earlier than bladder urges. While this may be frustrating, the solution is simple vigilance. Peeing is a more common urge, so you can focus on using your potty timer and doing preventive stops at the potty every 20 to 30 minutes.

Your son chooses to sit while peeing

This issue may happen, primarily after you have taught your son that he should sit while pooping. You can easily correct this problem by allowing him to watch his older brothers or dad while they pee. But this isn't a major issue. The important thing is getting the poop and pee into the toilet.

Your child is frightened of the big, bad toilet

The loud sound of the toilet flushing is often scary for some children. They may feel like it will suck them away just like it did their waste. You can assure them by allowing them to flush things down the toilet like pieces of toilet paper. Doing this will help reduce their fear and make them familiar with the sight and the sound of a flushing toilet.

Your child is experiencing a form of regression

Some children, after mastering potty training, may suddenly have issues with staying dry. Their accidents begin to increase, and it appears as though you didn't teach them anything. The truth is, stressful or strange events may trigger regression back to diapers. Common causes include moving into a new home, changing sleeping space, having a new baby, falling ill, or changing a daycare center.

Unpleasant things will arise as the journey of potty training advances. However, be confident that nothing can stop your child from being potty trained. How many adults do you know who can't use the bathroom? Everyone figures it out eventually. You can and will conquer all if you don't give up.

Keep Teaching

Learning something new requires diligence and commitment from both the person learning and the person teaching. Potty training is not the first (or last) skill that your child will get to learn from you. You are her constant teacher. You will continually help her acquire new skills, information, and behavior. You will influence her way of life.

When potty training your child, you must take advantage of various methods of teaching, including:

1. Giving clear instructions

You have to provide understandable explanations on what you want your kids to do and how you want them to do it.

Of course, this requires that you know those things in advance. So envision the result you desire and the steps required to get there.

Tips on giving your child potty training instructions:

- Ensure you have his full attention when you're teaching. Call him by name in between sentences and maintain eye contact as much as possible. This procedure will help get rid of distractions.

- Speak to him with a gentle and clear voice. Don't sound threatening or too stern, as this will only build fear around using the potty.

- Don't use complicated words to communicate the instructions. Instead, use words that are understandable for your child.

- Make use of illustrations and gestures that will make your point known and pass the message along.

- Ensure that your instruction is short and precise. Giving your child several instructions at one time may lead to him not getting anything from the talk at all.

Making use of a potty training poster will help your child remember the step-by-step instructions that you've given. This form of illustration will allow him to keep a firm grip on his training.

2. Serving as a model

A vital part of teaching and reinforcing is acting as an example. Being a role model is always useful when teaching your child to potty train.

Tips on modeling potty training skills:

- Ensure your child is paying attention to what you are showing her.

- Offer short comments in between actions to show her the vital parts of what you're doing. Making comments like "Look at me; I pee in here" or "See how I wash my hands after using the potty?" will also help.

- Show her the steps multiple times at a slow, easily comprehensible pace.

- Allow your child to practice what you just taught. For example, let her sit on the potty even when she is clothed to see what it feels like even if she doesn't want to try to pee or poop.

You may also want to break down the task into multiple steps, depending on how she is coping with what you have been training her. For example, you might want to teach her how to use the potty first and then how to wipe thoroughly or wash her hands properly. Having to break potty training into a series of actions may be stressful for you as the parent but it is a necessary sacrifice to help your child get the hang of potty training. As your child conquers a task, then you move on to the next one. When teaching the next step, review the first ones to show that everything works in a progression. It will also teach your child that one thing will lead to another. For example, pooping in the potty will require her to wipe her bottom and then wash her hands thoroughly.

3. Washing, flushing, and wiping

As we've discussed, the core lesson of potty training is peeing in the potty, rather than in the diapers. That is a tough enough concept for many toddlers to grasp. We've recommended that you hold off on your flushing and washing lectures if your child is wrestling with the core curriculum. Well, now that he's officially graduated from diapers, you can begin to teach those other important lessons.

Remember that you'll need to practice patience teaching these subjects too. Don't expect too much, and be sure to keep offering your praises and encouragements. Fortunately, these lessons a bit easier for most toddlers to grapple.

Other Considerations

Special Considerations for Boys

There is a gender consideration between girls and boys when it comes to potty training. What applies to the latter may not apply for the former. Many people believe that it takes a longer time to train boys than girls. This belief may be due to the fact that in the majority of cases, women get to potty train their children, which naturally privileges girl learners. It can also be associated with girls' natural instinct to be clean and tidy. Most girls don't like the feeling of being soiled and will usually have an intense desire for personal hygiene. These reasons do not mean, though, that boys cannot be potty trained successfully by their mommies. Knowing what to do will make the process easier.

Many parents are confused about whether to teach their boys to pee while standing or to start with sitting for the first part of potty training. Experts advise to teach them how to pee while sitting initially, as this will make them feel more familiar with the fundamentals. After you're sure that he has mastered that, then you can go on to teach him how to pee while standing and how to aim well.

Peeing in a standing position will come with challenges, as he will have to be taught not to make a mess while urinating. The best person to teach your son how to do it is the father as he has experienced the same thing when he was a child. Sometimes, there is an issue where boys have to distinguish when to stand and when to sit. You don't want your boy to try pooping in a standing position. It may be tricky to have to explain to him the difference between peeing and pooping.

Special Considerations for Girls

As mentioned, young girls naturally tend to get more sensitive to soiled diapers than boys. They may express their discomfort by yanking at their diapers or making weird faces. The way your child will show how she feels will be specific to her.

One way for your daughter to learn how to use the toilet is by letting her observe what you do. Also, your child will want to sit on the potty longer if she is comfortable. Look around your bathroom to ensure that the environment is comfortable for her.

Girls often love to have things look the way they want. You can give your daughter a chance to choose her own potty chair. Let her decorate it the way she wants with stickers and pictures of her favorite characters, like Dora or Barbie.

Most girls love looking nice and fancy. They enjoy playing dress up and looking pretty. As a parent, you can use this to your advantage by allowing her to dress herself, picking the underwear and outfit that she loves. Doing this will make her less likely to soil her clothing since she loves them and considers them pretty.

Girls are typically more concerned about cleanliness and hygiene than boys, and more expressive when they need to go. They will prefer to stop playing if it leaves them cleaner and with less mess.

A crucial thing to note when potty training girls is how to wipe. Girls are more susceptible to urinary tract infections than boys, and how they wipe is a chief cause. You must teach your child to wipe correctly from the front to the back. This precaution will serve to prevent infections in her bladder.

Girls are always big on imagination as well. For this reason, having a potty training doll that shows her why she needs to sit on the potty will be an excellent and effective learning tool for her. Your job is to make learning fun and as practical as possible.

When You Have to Be Away from Home

When you're going to be away, you have no choice but to break the progress you've painstakingly built. So, you have to prepare. One necessary step you can take is to ensure that your child visits the potty before you all finally walk out the door. Here are some helpful ideas:

Prepare the essentials

Take time to make a list of everything that you might need during your time away. If you doubt whether a particular item is necessary, err on the side of caution. The length of the journey will determine the amounts and types of the supplies you need. If you don't feel comfortable with your child having to use a public toilet seat, then you can bring along a travel potty seat. If you think that the journey will not permit potty breaks along the way, then you can put your child in diapers. However, keep in mind that it is only for the ride. As soon as you get to your destination, you should ask the child to slip on her underwear. Let her know that the diapers are only temporary and will be gone as soon as you get to where you are going.

Set a timer

When you're away, it's easy to forget all about potty breaks. To reduce the number of accidents that your child might have, you can set a timer to 30-minute intervals. This procedure will help alert you and serve as a reminder of regular potty breaks.

Different environments promote different behavior

Understand that being away from home may momentarily confuse your child. The scenery is new, and may distract him from his normal attention to his bodily functions. This does not mean that your training has been ineffective. Just get back on that horse and pick up where you left off.

What to Pack

Knowing what to pack will help you make the best of the situation. Here are some basic things to pack.

Change of Clothes

Packing a full change of clothes is a wise way to prepare for accidents. You should pack socks, underwear, shirt, shorts, and even shoes. If you're going to be out for more than an hour or two, why not pack a second set of clothes as well?

Antibacterial Wipes

This will come in handy more often than we can express.

Travel Potty

When away from home, bringing along a travel potty is also advised, for one simple reason: why the heck not? You have no way to determine the condition of the public toilets you'll have available or the number of stops you'll have to make. Having your potty with you will most likely turn out to be a life saver.

Disposable Toilet Seat Covers

As mentioned, public restrooms are often quite filthy. If you find yourself having to use one, it will help to have a barrier between your child's skin and that seat.

Piddle Pad

These are waterproof pads that minimize your number of accidents. You simply place them under your child to protect the car seat or restaurant chair from leaks.

Flushable Wipes

This is a type of wipe that you can flush down the toilet – friendly to most plumbing systems. With these, disposal is carefree. No worries of clogging.

Zip-Top Bags

This can help with storage purposes. You can keep dry or wet clothes in them in the event of an accident.

Potty Training Children with Special Needs

Most parents have stories about their potty training adventures. Some talk about the messes, the tantrums, or the ways their child resisted. Others talk about lost sleep and the slow progress. However, the story almost always ends happily – with a child who eventually became potty trained. However, there are some stories that don't have the same plot twists and endings. These are commonly the stories that pertain to children with disabilities.

There are many different types of developmental disorders, including cerebral palsy, mental retardation, Down syndrome, or autism, to name a few. Potty training children with special needs can prove to be more difficult. Most children reach the physical development necessary to be potty trained somewhere between the age of 18 months to about 2½ years. However, you cannot employ this rule when dealing with disabled kids. The reason is that a child with special needs may not be psychological or intellectually ready.

When potty training children with special needs, it is less important to focus on age. Rather, focus on where they are developmentally. How do you know when your child is developmentally prepared? You will need to be observant, watching for indications or signs.

For instance, does he feel uncomfortable and annoyed when wearing dirty diapers? Does he know when it's time to go? Does he follow basic instructions, and is he generally cooperative when it's time to go? Does he ask to wear underwear? Does he ask for the potty? A "yes" to these questions will help you feel more confident about being ready.

Of course, none of this will guarantee that your child will be ready, or that the process will go smoothly. Children with special needs may have a hard time getting to the potty on time or taking their clothes off. You will probably have to provide them with special tools like a stool or potty chair to make it easier for them.

In general, everything that we have already talked about should still apply to your special needs child. The techniques and procedures may just need some extra effort, additional patience, more forethought, and special techniques for motivating. Many of which, you may already use in your daily life as a parent.

Don't try to rush him – it won't accomplish anything other than give him unneeded pressure, which in turn may lead to emotional distress. And, as we've stated all along, the general rule applies that it's best not to potty train when you are preoccupied with other things.

One vital thing to remember is that children with special needs may need to use the potty more frequently. If you are able to notice patterns in your child, such as which time(s) of day she has been prone to soiling herself in the past, you can use this information to construct your routine. You can also get your child to sit on the potty after meals, as that's when she will most likely feel the urge to go.

One helpful alternative is to visit the potty only at times when your child wants to go, loosening up on the regimented 30 minute intervals. Doing so can help reinforce potty time as a positive experience and limit her frustrations. The reward system should provide additional motivation for her too.

Even after your child has seemingly mastered the art of potty training, it is not uncommon to see regression along the way. You shouldn't see this as resistance, but as signs that your child needs more training. Give her a lot of encouragement and praise for even small successes.

You must also pay careful attention to the sensory demands of your child. For example, she may react badly to certain smells or sounds. If so, you must try to accommodate her however you can. The key here is to stay encouraging. Always let her see that you appreciate her effort.

When Things Don't Go As Planned

When you're right in the thick of it, and there doesn't seem to be any apparent progress, you'll need a few pointers to help keep you balanced. They are:

Nakedness can be useful

Sometimes, being naked can help your child remember when it's time to go. You can pick certain hours of the day when you let him roam free and encourage him to sit on the potty. Although it will be messy if accidents occur, being naked can actually help prevent them, as it provides your child the constant reminder that he has somewhere to be when that old familiar need arises.

Combine fact with fiction

Another method you can try is attaching a fun story to your child about the potty. The good news is that it doesn't have to be true. He's a toddler. He's into fiction! You can tell him that the toilet is hungry and it needs something to eat. He may come to feel that his pooping in the bathroom is an act of giving. Go ahead. Use your imagination. I'm sure you'll be able to come up with a "white lie" that excites him about the adventures of potty training.

Identifying the source of the problem

Many times, a technique's lack of success is due to a child's unspoken fear. She may be afraid of sitting on the big, scary toilet seat or hate to see her poop get flushed away. Whatever it is, you will be able to make significant strides if you can identify (and address) the source of the problem.

Taking advantage of social cues

Children are challenged when they see their peers doing something. It can make them want to prove themselves and let others see that they are just as capable. You can use this to your advantage. Point out to your child how her friends use the potty when they feel the need to go. Point out how big and brave they are for doing this. This will help her not only realize the need to use the potty, but also fuel a desire to copy her friends' actions.

Conclusion

So, you've arrived at the end. Do you feel ready? Hopefully, we've done a fair job at prepping you with enough helpful information for the job. If you need more, however, or if you'd like a refresher, the 25 helpful bonus tips at the end of this book should add a few extra tasty tidbits to your plate. Some of them will be refreshers. Others will offer new information.

At this point, you should have a decent idea about what this process will require, as well as a basic format of the plan that you have in mind. You've thought about some of the products you may need, as well as where you can go to look for them.

You know that it's not going to be a cakewalk. You know that encouragement and patience will be required – both for you and your child.

You fully understand that this will not be a time for multitasking, or trying to balance multiple work and home projects simultaneously. You know that you'll have to give this your undivided focus – probably, taking at least 3 days off of work.

You know that preparation is required – even outside of buying the right equipment. You should have books and songs ready. You should have a log template made for any recording of data that you think will be helpful. You should have all the knickknacks and extras that will make your job easier, as well as improve your overall chances at success.

You know that you should become familiar with the lingo – the correct terminology for this short phase of life, which your child will be able to relate with and which you will be able to make yourself clear with.

You know that you should be mentally prepared as well, having built up a reservoir of all the necessary patience, perseverance, and determination that will be required. And, you know that you should be prepared to push on through sentimental feelings that create a resistance to change.

You know that starting means a brand new chapter. It's bye-bye to diapers. There is no coming back. Once you begin, it's game time baby. The only way forward is to go ALL the way. No halftimes, test runs, or partial efforts. If you're doing this, you're doing this. That's that.

You know about the importance of keeping your child well-hydrated, so that he regularly experiences the urge to go. You know that you can't wait for her to ask. You have to be the one to lead on this journey.

You know that you should reinforce good habits as often as possible, celebrating each success with praises, encouragements, and even rewards (while not overdoing it). You know about the importance of staying sincere in your praise – using it as a tool to communicate positive truths, rather than as a mechanism for manipulation.

You know that you should get others involved – your husband, your older kids, your sister in law, or your mom. Whoever is there (and who your child knows) can contribute to your youngster's success, and play a vital role in a process that can (and should) be memorable.

You know about naps and bedtime – that they both come add certain challenges. You know that more will be required of you during these times, and you're prepared to even lose a little sleep in order to wake your child up and avoid messes.

You know what to do and what not to do – the common pitfalls and advantages. And,, you understand the importance of constantly reinforcing – even after you've reached your goal.

You know how to prepare yourself for those moments when you'll be away from home. A disrupted routine doesn't mean potty training is over. It means you keep going, even in new situations and surroundings. The game isn't called on a count of rain!

Finally, you know what to do when things don't go as planned. You don't give into despair or put the plan on hold for another year. You don't sulk in self-pity or compare yourself to your sister. You keep a stiff upper lip and say, "Well, I guess that's life." Then, you carry on just as you had been.

That is what you know, and that is what makes you ready.

25 Bonus Tips

1. **Connect with others**

Look for people who are in the same boat as you. They will be in the know and capable of providing information that is helpful. And, they may have resources that you need. You may even be able to collaborate on certain matters. Never a bad thing to have somebody by your side, eh? Chances are, she'll feel the same way!

2. **Look for the signs of readiness**

Timing is a crucial factor. A good way to make both you and your child miserable is by trying to force the process. Instead, know when she is ready. Here are some signs and indications that can help determine this:

- they show interest in underwear, the toilet, or bathroom,
- they want to watch how you or older siblings use the toilet,
- they poop during easily predictable times,

- they remain dry for two hours or more,
- they pull off their pants and put them back on,
- they adhere to simple instructions,
- they understand and respond to potty language, or
- they always ask for a change of diapers whenever they are soiled or wet.

3. Let them choose which "big kid pants" they want to wear

Allowing your child to pick his underwear will make him more careful about soiling it. Giving him the freedom to choose what he wears will increase his attachment to it. It is the nature of children to protect what they love.

4. Utilize the power of choice

It is in both of your interests not to make this process into a power struggle. To avoid that, pay close attention to how your words are structured. Try not to make your child feel like he is being forced. Make your statements sound more like gentle instructions or challenges. Try to say "Let's go potty" or "I bet you know how to use the potty chair now."

You may choose to offer some choices, such as which bathroom he can use, whether he'll use a soap dispenser or bar soap to wash his hands, or which book he prefers you to read him while he's going potty. Utilize the power of choice. It can be a very positive thing.

5. Have a reward system

Knowing your child's likes and preferences is crucial; it will help you determine what to give him for his successes. You don't want to motivate him with things that have no value to him. He'll feel far more more motivated if you speak his language. The more effort and thought you put into his rewards, the closer you will be to pleasing him.

6. Be careful with the sweets

As much as possible, avoid giving sugary and high-calorie foods as a reward. Eating habits tend to form at an early age. Too many sweets could start your youngster off in the wrong direction. It could also cause him to bounce off the walls while he's supposed to be napping. Neither of these are good scenarios. Also, consider that unhealthy foods negatively impact digestion, which can have adverse effects on your short-term potty training efforts.

This doesn't mean that you can't offer your child any sweets. It just means that you should keep a level head about it. Don't raise the roof too high when your kid gets it right. Have a celebration that fits the occasion.

7. Keep on the funny side

Potty training is as fun as you make it. Fortunately, there are plenty of occasions to laugh as you go about it. Because, after all… why not? It will be over before you know it. Lean towards laughter and keep a positive perspective. You'll find that you've managed to make good memories where you weren't expecting them.

8. Keep yourself encouraged

It's very easy to forget about one important thing during this whole process – you. You need encouragement. You need pats on the back. You need chocolate moose tracks ice cream from time to time too, so be sure to keep your own motivational tank filled. And, be sure to do it regularly, because you don't want to run out of steam during key moments.

9. Limit toilet paper

Children love to play with things that amuse them, especially the ones that are in motion. Unspooling the toilet paper looks like a fun task, and your child will *love* to overdo it. It's always good to draw a line on the wall under the toilet paper to mark how long each strand should be. This precaution will prevent them from clogging the toilet with excess paper and making a huge mess.

10. Expect a difference between nighttime and daytime training

It is normal for children to have issues with controlling their bladder at night – even after mastering daytime potty training. Positive progress in one area does not guarantee good results in the other. They are two very different animals. To help, you can make use of waterproof mattress covers, overnight training pants, or any of the other myriad useful inventions designed to make potty training easier. Your child will catch onto night training eventually. It may be sometime after you've successfully potty trained her during the day.

11. Ask questions

Try to engage your child in conversations. Get to know what is going on in her mind. Understand her desires, her reluctance, and her reasoning. This will be your best tool for finding solutions. It's one thing to observe your child's behavior; it's another thing to become familiar with what's behind it. You can do this by asking her specific questions, and being a safe enough place for her to give sincere answers.

12. Expect the unexpected

No one probably has to tell you this, but you should prepare yourself for the unexpected – especially when your routine is broken by travel, sickness, or emergencies. Try to see surprises – not as signs of failure, but as perfect opportunities for you to teach (and learn).

13. Prepare for boredom

You probably don't like to sit in the bathroom for extended periods of time, and neither will your child. You will probably get bored. Try to see this as a great opportunity to read potty training stories, which should help turn that monotony into fun time!

14. The flush may be too much

During the early stages of potty training, it is normal for your child not to fully grasp the concept of flushing, or to understand that this is part of the job. That's okay. It'll come in time. For now, focus on getting the main goal mastered. You can worry about the details after that.

15. Don't expect perfection

Don't expect perfection from both yourself or your child. Expecting perfection will only cause you frustration, because things probably aren't going to go exactly as you like. Your mindset plays an important role in the process.

16. Consider your child's uniqueness

No two children are the same. Your child is nothing like your sister's child or your best friend's child or even your mother's child (you). Why is this worth mentioning? Because it will help you pay close attention to what sets your child apart. The more you are aware of your child's uniqueness, the more patience you'll have, and the better you'll be able to customize a potty training plan for him.

17. Be prepared for the stubborn or strong-willed child

In some cases, children put up various kinds of resistance during potty training. They may refuse to get on the potty or put on their underwear or follow basic instructions. In such situations, the solution is not to show anger or disdain, but to stay centered. If possible, put off positive vibes and focus on reinforcing the good behavior. Over time, the behavior that you reward is the behavior that will continue.

18. Use a timeline for goal setting and consistency

It's impossible to know how much progress you're making if you have no way to measure it. A timeline can help you determine if you're where you thought you'd be at specific moments. Just be careful not to go too far with this idea. You don't want to be a buzzkill by setting deadlines on every small detail. Just try to mark the significant goals as key milestones.

19. Add food coloring to the toilet water to make it fun

You may also try adding food coloring to the toilet water to make peeing more fun. Your child will be fascinated by the way that the toilet water changes color when he pees.

20. Incorporate music

Remember that making potty training a time for songs and laughter is a good way to make your child see this process as a fun, exciting thing. Making it lively for him will ensure a more positive outcome.

21. Wake them at night

While it's true that interrupting your child's sleep may make her tired the next day, it's also true that **not** waking her up will lead to frequent accidents. The key is to find a balance. It is recommended to wake her up once or at most twice within a night for potty breaks, but no more than that.

22. Read as much as you can

There are many resources and tools available online to prepare you for potty training. This includes (but is not limited to) books, articles, and even educational videos to better equip you with what to do at each stage of the journey. Remember that you're learning not just for yourself, but also for your child.

23. Don't offer a diaper for poop

It's common during potty training for your child to request diapers when she has to poop. But, this is not a good idea. Your child needs to understand that her waste must always go in the toilet. Be firm, but be gentle and kind in your instructions. Don't give into her desires for comfort and familiarity.

24. Use stickers and fun visuals

Colors and images are excellent learning tools for children. Colorful things help them assimilate knowledge better than words alone. They may easily become bored with the whole potty training experience. Placing colorful stickers at strategic points in the house where your child can easily spot them will help bring fun into the learning. Remember that your method of training matters. Being a good teacher means knowing how to make the learning process both fun and enlightening for your little student.

25. Grab a stool

Most times, children have a hard time reaching the adult-sized toilet. You can resolve this by placing a stool at the bottom of the toilet. It also serves as a brace for him when he wants to poop. Note – he may not be used to this, but it will prove helpful, as he needs all the support and stability he can get. The more comfortable he is, the longer he can sit on the potty.

References

Hall, S. (2018, August 6). The Dangers Of Early Potty Training. Retrieved from https://www.allaboutincontinence.co.uk/blog/dangers-early-potty-training

Robock, K. (2018, July 5). 6 Worst Mistakes Parents Make When Trying 3-day Potty Training. Retrieved from https://www.todaysparent.com/toddler/potty-training/6-worst-mistakes-parents-make-when-trying-3-day-potty-training/

Made in the USA
Columbia, SC
01 June 2020